D0328113

Plants That Eat Bugs

by Liz Ray

Some bugs eat plants.
The bugs eat the leaves.

Some plants eat bugs!

Snap!

Look at the leaves
on this plant.
They can trap bugs.
A bug lands on a leaf,
and the leaf snaps shut.
Snap!

The leaf traps the bug.
The bug can not get out.
Then the plant can eat
the bug.

Stick!

The leaves on this plant
are sticky.
A bug lands on a leaf,
and the bug sticks to it.
Stick!

The leaf rolls up.
The leaf traps the bug.
The bug can not get out.
Then the plant can eat
the bug.

The leaves on this plant
look like cups.
The cups are traps
for bugs!

The cups have smooth sides.
A bug lands in a cup,
and it slides down.
Slide!

The plant traps the bug
inside the cup.
Then the plant can eat
the bug.

How do these plants get bugs?

Snap!

Stick!

Slide!

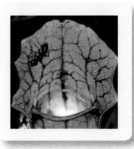